33 WAYS NOT TO
SCREW UP YOUR BUSINESS
EMAILS

ANNE JANZER

CONTENTS

INTRODUCTION

Emails are the one type of business writing that every one of us does. Yet we all have room to improve. We dash them off without much thought, and sometimes suffer the consequences.

Take a good, hard look at your email inbox. It's probably a mix of important conversations, things you're putting off reading, and tasks you simply don't want to deal with. How much of it do you read carefully?

Many people say email is broken, or archaic, or a drain on productivity. Yet it shows no indication of going away, and with the growth of remote work it may only be increasing.

When you send a message, you launch it into a digital torrent of words, all clamoring for attention in someone's inbox. Your challenge is to get your message across by rising above the sea of poorly thought-out, hastily composed emails.

When email is less effective, we must be *more* effective in how we use it.

GETTING IT WRONG VS. GETTING IT RIGHT

Effective email practices can boost your career. Sloppy email habits might crater it.

The world is filled with email mishaps and misfires. You'll find many of them in these pages, along with advice for protecting yourself from them.

But you can do better than simply avoiding mistakes. You can write emails that people want to open, that they find valuable and refer back to. As long as email is with us in the business world, those who master it have a real advantage:

- Better collaboration with colleagues
- Greater success when sending queries or asking for input or responses
- A reputation for clarity of thought and expression

HOW TO USE THIS BOOK

This is not a book of email templates or what *words* to write, although you'll find examples for clarity. Instead, it's about email *practices*. It highlights 33 common mistakes, while offering suggestions on how to build practices that set you up for success rather than failure.

The practices in this book represent the combined wisdom of legions of people—authors, researchers, consultants, and other professionals—who responded to my requests for advice and stories.

If you're just getting started in the corporate world, absorb this advice and you'll stand out from the pack. If you've been working for a long time or if you find yourself swamped in email and relying on it more than before, search the book for topics that catch your interest. You may find ideas and practices here you want to add to your repertoire, elevating your email effectiveness.

As a bonus, the skills you develop and hone writing emails will show up in every other aspect of your business writing life, including social media posts, blog posts, reports, and more. And as the workplace reshapes itself with more remote work and virtual collaboration, writing skills are becoming more important than ever before.

Emails are an opportunity to cultivate clarity of thought and expression. They give us a chance to practice our writing skills, every darned day. Let's start.

#1 UNNECESSARY EMAILS

What's your point? The simplest way to be a good email citizen is to use it thoughtfully; don't contribute to the noise needlessly. Make sure your messages serve a purpose, for both you and the recipient. Think before you type.

Before you fire off an email, whether to your manager or team or to an outside customer, client, or partner, try to answer these questions:

- What are you trying to communicate? If you're not crystal clear on the takeaway, you cannot expect someone else to understand what you mean.
- Why will someone read it? Why will they spend a few precious moments of their attention on this email? If you can't answer that, rethink the email.
- What do you hope they will do? Will they understand that after reading the message?

When you think clearly about your purpose, you can identify who should and should not receive the email. You can include only the information supporting that purpose and leave the rest aside, getting to the point quickly. And, you can make it easy for the recipient to respond in the appropriate way. People will appreciate this.

FIRST PURPOSE, THEN CONTENTS

Writing is a window into thinking. If your thoughts are muddled and disorganized, your writing will be as well.

We tend to start typing an email message as soon as thoughts enter our head, which generates a one-sided conversation. Your initial train of thought may not be the best way to communicate with someone else. Some people juggle hundreds of incoming emails every day, all while ostensibly doing their job. Mold the message to your purpose by planning before you write.

FIND THE GOLDILOCKS ZONE

One friend told me in frustration that no one on her team did emails right. Of the three people on her team, one writes emails that are way too long with unnecessary details. Another sends short messages lacking the necessary information, generating multiple follow-up messages. A third writes emails that are the right length, but don't cover the right things.

They were all missing the "Goldilocks" zone—just the right amount of information to serve the purpose.

Where do your messages fall on the Goldilocks scale? Too much? Too little? Just right?

Before you write your next high-stakes email, sketch out your purpose and identify exactly what you need to include to achieve that purpose. When that purpose is in hand, you can safely start writing.

A WRITING PROCESS TIP

For important messages, write the first draft somewhere other than the email software. Start earlier—ideally the day before, but an hour before if that's all you've got. Use software like Word or Google Docs to get your thoughts out of your head. Then pick the key elements that will serve the purpose in the email. Rearrange them. Revise and edit until you're comfortable with the result. Then, and only then, should you paste it into the email message.

- Writing outside of the email software removes the pressure to come up with perfect words. It gives you permission to think and write more freely.
- This practice also prevents you from sending your muddled, half-cooked ideas out into the world, either accidentally or in a moment of impatience. (*I'm going to hit Send and be done with this!*)

#2 FORMALITY FAILURES

Have you ever received a casual, flippant email from someone you don't know? Depending on your mood or situation, you might either smile or feel annoyed.

In the other extreme, what happens if you get a super-formal email from a close friend or colleague? If it's a friend, you wonder if their account has been hacked. If it came from your manager, you worry about your future employment status.

Email has unspoken rules of etiquette, and many of them have to do with how formal or informal the message is.

Before you write an email, understand where it falls on the "informal/formal" spectrum, based on your relationship with the recipient and the purpose and context of the message. This simple decision will affect many things, including the salutation and sign-off, the use of punctuation and emojis, and how long the message should be. Figure it out *before* you start writing, especially to a new email correspondent or someone you don't yet know.

HOW FORMAL DO YOU NEED TO BE?

There are no hard-and-fast rules for business emails, because email replaces *both* formal and informal communications.

Remember faxes? And when's the last time you wrote a formal business letter that you posted in the mail? When email first arrived in the business world, we thought it would replace those ponderous paper communications. It has done that, and more.

Soon it expanded to absorb a whole bunch of communication tasks, and it's only grown since then. It reminds me of the farmer who brought European rabbits to Australia for hunting, only to find that they reproduced like, well, rabbits and disrupted the ecosystem.

Email has done something similar for our professional lives, crowding out other communication channels, including:

- Conversations that once happened in person or by phone
- Letters and forms with transactional information (Now we send emails saying *I received the package*)
- Formal requests or legal permissions (Today: *With this email, I acknowledge that ...*)

Because of the many roles they fill, emails can range from quite informal (replacing quick conversations and texts) to the most formal (business letters, legal documents, and so on).

Most emails fall somewhere in the middle. When searching for the right level, consider the purpose of the email, the recipient's style, and the context of your relationship.

Purpose: If you are sending an official request for a transfer or contract amendment, opt for a formal tone. For a fleeting conversation with friendly colleagues, you might load up with emojis and exclamation points, and use inside jokes that only your team knows.

Personal preferences: People tend to gravitate to one side or the other of the formality spectrum. For some, email is an extension of texting, while others craft carefully scripted business letters. If you know someone's preferences, lean in that direction.

Cultural preferences: When emailing people in other countries or cultures, remember that what works for your team may seem abrupt to others. According to Lanie Denslow, principal of World Wise Intercultural Training, "For most cultures, the relationship is at the heart of doing business." With that in mind, you may want to start with a personal question or common interest before jumping into the "business" of the message. Ask about their local news or the results of a past interaction. A sentence or two can communicate that you think of them as more than simply a source of information or a means to an end.

Relationship: Consider both familiarity and the balance of power in your relationship with the person you're emailing.

How well do you know the recipient? If you've worked closely together, a formal email might make them worry.

Does the person have the upper hand in your relationship? If so, tip toward the more formal side of the spectrum. You probably won't send a super-informal *Hey!* to the CEO of a Fortune 500 company unless you know them personally.

Conversely, if you are in a position of power over the other person (say, they report to you regularly), an unusually formal tone may set off alarms. (*Why are they being so formal? Am I about to be let go?*)

If you don't know the recipient well, here are a few safe strategies:

- Have you communicated with them before? If so, mirror the formality of past emails, paying attention to how they open and conclude them.
- If not, err on the side of caution and be more formal than you think necessary. If you receive a lively response riddled with exclamation points, you can relax in the next email. It's easier to dial the formality back than to add it once you've started an exchange.
- Remember what you were taught as a child: *please* and *thank you* never offend.

#3 SALUTATIONS: YOU LOST ME AT HELLO

How do you start that email? Do you tend toward a formal salutation (*Dear Anne*) or start with the person's name by itself? Do you jump right into the content without any greeting?

My own email inbox illustrates a range of options, including: *Hi, Anne*; *Hello, Anne*; *Greetings, Anne*; *Dear Anna* (wrong name); *Hi there*; *Hey!*

More than 500 people responded to a survey I ran on LinkedIn. Over half chose *Hi name* as their preferred greeting, with 20 percent at *Hello name*, and 12 percent using *Dear name*.

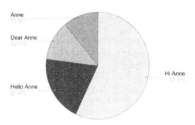

There are other options.

- A few people told me they like *Hey* for informal communications. Others said that it sounded either surprised or dismissive. (*Hey, cat, get off the bed!*)
- The use of *Dear* generates mixed feelings. Some people find it awkwardly formal, others think it's charming. One person in India found it the only safe choice.

There's no single right answer. As always, it depends on your style and your relationship with the recipient. The greeting sets the tone for the rest of the email.

Hey is least formal, *Hi* slightly more so, *Hello* still more. At the most-formal end of the spectrum is *Dear name*. Getting that name right is its own challenge, described below.

Some people dispense with the salutation altogether and jump right into the content. While that's fine if you're continuing a conversation in an email thread, I suggest you include a greeting when starting a new thread, even if it is merely the recipient's name.

WHY YOU SHOULD LEAD WITH THE RECIPIENT'S NAME

There's a reason that so many of the marketing emails you receive start with your first name. Email marketers test these things, and the name makes a difference.

We are wired to pay attention to our names. If someone mentions our name within earshot in a crowded room, it is likely to grab our attention. Psychologists call this the *cocktail party effect*. Research shows that the same thing happens in print.

Adding a name is also considerate. Have you ever started reading an email without a salutation and wondered why you were getting it, before noticing that you were cc'd on the message but not the main recipient? Spare your reader that potential confusion.

When we see our own name, we know at a glance that the email is directed to us. Seeing someone else's name in the greeting is likewise helpful. Of course, people can check the email header to see how it was routed, but why make them do that? They might be distracted while glancing quickly through their inbox.

My friend Catherine Johns, a professional speaker, bypasses the greeting altogether, jumping right into the email message while carefully using the recipient's name in the first sentence. Her example: *Your email delighted me, Leslie.*

If you're addressing a group, make that clear in the greeting, in a style consistent with your familiarity with others and the corporate culture: *Hi, team.*

GET THE NAME RIGHT

Do you use the person's first name, or do you go for a title or Mr. or Ms.? Or something else? The name can be a minefield when communicating with people in different cultures.

Make sure you know someone's preferred pronouns (she/her, he/him, they) or gender identity if you add a gender-specific designation like Mr. or Ms. You may also have to figure out which name is the surname. A few moments of research can save you from embarrassment.

WHAT TO DO WHEN YOU DON'T KNOW THE NAME

Sometimes you need to send a message to a general email account (Support@ or Hiring@) rather than an individual. You know it's a real person on the other end and want to be human. How do you start that email?

Again, it depends on the formality of the situation.

Don't use *Dear Sir* or assume anything about the gender of the recipient. *Dear Sir or Madam* isn't much better. I don't know many women who respond well to *Madam*. *To whom it may concern* sounds formal and distant. If you're angry at the organization you're contacting, you might lead with that. They'll get the message.

To convey a friendlier tone, consider including the title or role of the person you hope reads the email: *Dear Acme Support Team* might work, or *To the hiring manager at Acme.*

THE UNUSUAL SALUTATION

You'll find all kinds of greetings in your emails, especially if you follow creative writers and marketers, as I do. While working on this chapter, I received an email that starts *Hey Go-Getter!*

With email greetings, context is everything. If people have a clear idea of your personality, then you can use unusual greetings that are consistent with your personal brand. The wonderful author and marketer Ann Handley can start an email with "What's up, buttercup?" and I read it with eagerness.

If you are a master of tone, go for it, but realize that strangers and people who value formality may be put off. Otherwise, stick with a greeting that matches your style and doesn't annoy your recipient.

IF IN DOUBT, MIRROR

The most important factor is what the recipient expects. If the person you are sending to regularly uses wacky or creative greetings, you can respond with one of your own. If they default to a formal salutation, do something similar.

#4 VERBAL VIRTUOSITY

Let's imagine that you're sending an email to a team you have just joined. You think this is your chance to introduce everyone to your brilliance and wisdom.

You pull out all the stops. You use five-syllable words and an elaborate sentence structure that would make your college writing professor swoon, demonstrating mastery of dependent clauses and intricacies of thought.

Stop! Resist the urge to dazzle.

Email is not the place to show off. Your eloquent wording will probably fail to impress the recipient, who may glance at it while riding a subway. Worse, it can work against you.

Trying to sound smart often backfires, making people think *less* of you. (There's a marvelous study on the topic titled "Consequences of erudite vernacular utilized irrespective of necessity: problems with using long words needlessly." Look it up.)

It all comes down to a concept called *cognitive load*.

Cognitive load is the amount of work happening in the reader's working memory to make sense of what you've written. It's like an extra mental tax added to the job of reading and handling emails. If you load up your message with complex sentences and big words to sound smart, you're adding to the reader's load.

- Unfamiliar words make people stop in their tracks to figure out the meaning. (*What does "intransigent" mean again?*) Now part of their mental energy is devoted to decoding the word rather than focusing on your message. That's a cognitive tax.
- When readers encounter long, complex sentences, they have to juggle the clauses in their heads until they reach the end of the sentence. That's another cognitive tax.

People often read emails in small slivers of time, when their attention is already scarce. They may check their email under the table or out of view of the camera during a boring meeting or while waiting in line for coffee. They don't have a lot of attention to spend deconstructing your prose.

Every rhetorical flourish opens up the possibility of a misunderstanding. Maybe someone won't make it through that long and elegant sentence. They'll misinterpret what you've written.

Unless you are confident that people will closely analyze every sentence, email is not the place for verbal virtuosity.

Instead, impress your colleagues with your clarity and ability to get to the heart of the matter. People will think better of you because you use their time well. If your emails are diffi-cult to slog through, reading them will feel like a chore. That's probably not the "personal brand" you hope to develop on the job.

#5 WRITING LIKE AN INSIDER: JARGON

Ah, jargon. We love to complain when it comes from *other* people. Yet we often don't even notice that we're using it ourselves. That obliviousness can hurt us.

First, let's take a moment to define what we mean by *jargon*. Jargon consists of industry terminology, acronyms, and abbreviations that:

- Are unfamiliar to people outside of a specific company, industry, or area of expertise
- Can be replaced with other, more widely accessible terms

Not all industry terminology qualifies as jargon. We may use precise, technical terms in our jobs. These terms save time when communicating with people who share the same professional language.

For example, someone who installs heating, ventilation, and air conditioning systems will use the term *HVAC* when interacting with peers or suppliers. But the homeowner, sweltering in a house during a heat wave, is looking for the words *air conditioner* or *cooling*.

A term becomes jargon when it appears in front of someone who does not know it, or for whom it is not instantly familiar. Industry terminology has a social context, which we may forget when communicating with mixed audiences.

JARGON AS "INSIDER" LANGUAGE

We use language to form connections with people in groups. In that sense, jargon reinforces a sense of community. Go ahead, use the code word for your new project when emailing your team, for example. It builds cohesion.

Using jargon is a way of claiming insider status. And when you're an insider, someone else becomes an outsider.

If your email will travel beyond your group, replace terms that require insider knowledge or understanding with more accessible ones. Dial back the jargon to avoid confusion, and to protect your career. When you leave out the jargon, people who are new to the group or unfamiliar with the language will feel more welcome. They are also more likely to understand the message.

THE HIDDEN COSTS OF JARGON

Imagine that you're sending an email to a prospective customer about your services or solutions. To show the depth of your knowledge, you load it up with industry terminology.

Let's look at what might happen when the prospect reads it.

- If they don't know a word, they might spend time looking it up or asking people. Or they might continue without understanding your meaning. Neither is a good outcome. *Cost: wasted time.*

- Even if readers have seen a term before, they will be distracted for a moment while remembering what it means. You've lost their focus and added to the cognitive load mentioned in the last chapter. *Cost: lost attention.*
- Encountering unfamiliar words makes the reader subtly aware of the fact that they are on the outside. It's like shutting a door in their face. *Cost: emotional distance.*

That sounds like a recipe for a lost sale or damaged working relationship.

What if you're communicating with colleagues, partners, or experts? Surely it's okay to use the "insider" words to signal your expertise?

Not necessarily. You should still take the time to prune the jargon. Although you may imagine that the vocabulary makes you look like an adept insider, it could signal insecurity. According to a study titled "Compensatory Conspicuous Communication," people in lower-status positions use more jargon than their higher-status counterparts.

Your fancy words may be making you look insecure.

QUICK FIX: SCAN AND CAN THE JARGON

Unfortunately, insider language quickly becomes second nature. We're surrounded by people using the language of our company or industry, and forget that it is less familiar to others. That's due to the Curse of Knowledge: we forget what it's like to not know the things we know.

When emailing people outside your company (especially

customers, clients, or prospects), check carefully for words and acronyms that might be unfamiliar.

Where possible, replace the jargon with a simpler, more accessible term. If you can't replace it, consider defining it quickly. Spell out acronyms the first time you use them.

If you're not sure whether a term is jargon, try sending the email to a trusted colleague or friend first—someone not in your specific industry—and ask them if it could be clearer.

Yes, this does require you to find alternative wording. But it's worth doing, as your reputation is at stake. People admire those who clarify situations and topics, and avoid people who make them feel like outsiders.

#6 OVERPACKING EMAILS

I once worked with a client for years before we met in person. He lived on the East Coast and preferred to communicate by phone. Living in California, I favored email, partly because of time zone issues. I'd compile a list of questions for him at the end of my day and send them in an email, hoping he would answer in his morning, three hours ahead of Pacific Time.

Inevitably, he responded by answering only the first question on the list. Only one.

The next day, we'd get on the phone to sort through the remaining questions.

It took me a while to realize that he wasn't actively ignoring my questions. This was simply how he handled email. Once he read the first question and knew the answer, he'd hit *Reply*. I made the (repeated) mistake of sending him an over-packed email. It didn't work for him, just as it doesn't work for many people. I soon learned to include only one question per email.

That was years ago. Today, our email boxes are overflowing. Even a word-loving person like myself shudders at a long email message, knowing that I'll have to give it my full and precious attention.

If you have a lot to communicate, make it as easy as possible for the recipient to handle, store, or respond to your messages.

BREAK IT UP

If you want to cover multiple topics, consider sending shorter, single-subject emails. Many people use their inboxes as a virtual filing cabinet. Single-subject emails are less likely to get lost in the clutter. And you'll get a much better response from people like my former client.

START WITH A SUMMARY AND LABEL IT

If the message covers a lot of ground, start with a summary before getting to the details. Some people won't get further than the summary. If it catches their interest, they can continue to the details.

Use subheads to label the summary and details: this aids people who skim, whether by choice or necessity.

SEPARATE THE REQUEST FROM THE REASONING

When we're speaking in person, we often start with the reasons, and then ask for a favor or action. But with email, if you start with the reasons, the reader may not even get to the request. Start with the request, so they can clearly spot it.

For the sake of the burdened reader, make the request first. Then give a reason. For example:

> *Please send any comments you have on the draft by Tuesday, the 12th, at 5pm.*

We plan to publish by the end of Wednesday, and I need time to integrate your comments and proofread the result.

You don't need to offer a whole list of reasons: one will suffice. In research conducted by Ellen Langer at Harvard University, participants asking to cut in line to use a copy machine had better success when they offered a reason, even a lame one. The study demonstrates that people are more likely to grant you a favor if you give them a reason of any kind.

USE SUBHEADS OR FORMATTING TO ADD CLARITY

If an email message includes multiple topics or sections, formatting helps the reader make sense of it. Try adding a short, bold subheading before each section. Bullet points help people skim lists.

Formatting is a navigation aid for the reader—especially for those skimming through the email in stolen moments of their day. It only takes a few moments to elevate the impact of your email.

Your recipients will appreciate the effort.

QUICK FIX: USE AN ATTACHMENT

If you must communicate a pile of detailed information, consider creating a separate document and adding it as an attachment.

We treat attachments differently than the body of the message. We read them with more care. We might print or download and save them. The attachment strategy works well for documents like project proposals, detailed meeting notes, and complicated instructions.

At the same time, summarize the information in the body of the email, for those who put off reading the attachment.

#7 IGNORING PERSONAL PREFERENCES

Email is not everyone's favorite way to communicate. For many, it is a necessary evil. Some people feel unrelenting stress from an inbox constantly crying out for attention. The last thing you want to do to your colleagues is to make them dread hearing from you.

If you interact with someone regularly, learn their email and communication preferences. And if you don't know, ask. Even if you cannot accommodate them completely, asking is considerate.

Frequency: How frequently do they want to receive emails from you? Ask a manager or coworker whether they would prefer project updates through daily conversations, daily or weekly email updates, or any other form.

Format: If you need a quick answer to a question, how would they like you to ask them? Email, text, collaboration/message software like Microsoft Teams or Slack?

Similarly, let the people you work with know your preferences. If you prefer texting over email, tell people why: you don't want the message to get lost in your inbox, for example. If you lean toward email and have a text-dependent colleague, offer to text them when sending an important email that needs their attention.

For example, my coaching clients sometimes want to coordinate our work using text messages or real-time messaging applications. That's fine with me, but I always clarify expectations of responsiveness: *I'm happy communicating by text, as long as you realize that I may not respond right away. I need time to compose my thoughts.*

Honor and work with the expectations of your colleagues.

#8 THE TOO-SHORT MESSAGE

Perhaps you skimmed over chapter #6 on overpacked emails thinking, *I always write short emails. Everyone must love mine.*

Not so fast.

Brevity is golden, but it's not always appreciated. Even assuming you can communicate your message, your time-saving approach may offend, bewilder, or worry the recipient.

Here are three situations in which super-brief messages could damage your reputation and work relationships.

1. Lack of familiarity: How do you feel if a stranger comes up to you and asks you to do something? That feels either like a hard sell or an imposition. Your delightfully concise email can have the same effect if you don't know the recipient well.

If it's your first email to someone, remind them of your relationship or why you're reaching out. For example:

We met at the conference last month, and you gave me your card in case I wanted to connect.

2. Power imbalance: What would you do if you received an email like this from your manager one evening: *Let's talk in the morning. – Sam*

Gah! You might not sleep well. Is it good news? Bad news? What the heck?

If there's a power imbalance in the relationship, efficient and concise prose may come across as cryptic, abrupt, or worrisome.

3. Different cultural norms: Expectations for length and politeness vary among people, organizations, and nations. When sending an email to a colleague with a formal business culture, follow a template for a formal email:

- A full salutation (such as *Dear name*)
- A description of who you are in relationship to that individual
- The purpose of the email
- A respectful conclusion (thanking them for their help)
- Your full name

In subsequent exchanges on the email chain, let the other person demonstrate how brief you can be.

QUICK FIX: MIRROR THE RECIPIENT

When in doubt, look at any emails you have from the recipient or anyone like them. Do they open with "small talk" or polite exchanges? If so, try something similar, even if it's shorter. Do they include personal well wishes for your family? If it feels appropriate, do the same.

You are unlikely to insult someone by mirroring their email behavior.

#9 SETTING THE WRONG TONE

People I don't know often send emails asking me to review their books. One time, I responded by declining with a polite message of support and good wishes. Or so I thought.

Apparently, this author didn't feel the same. He sent a hurt and angry reply about my rude and dismissive response. I was mortified. Instead of letting it drop, I responded again, clarifying my intentions. He replied, saying he'd been in a bad mood and could see how that had affected his interpretation. It worked out okay in the end. But it made me wonder: how many times has a seemingly innocent email provoked this kind of reaction without my knowing it?

Emails are like little robot emissaries that we send out in the world on our behalf to ask people to pay attention. They cannot replace us. We can put smiley emojis in them, but emails do not smile. They do not comfort, show respect, or encourage. The person reading them must reconstruct the tone using what's on the screen, without our in-person cues. And many variables can influence their interpretation: lack of attention, a bad mood, fatigue, hunger, past experiences, and more.

A study published in the *Journal of Personality and Social Psychology* suggests that people misinterpret the tone of emails about half the time. Yes, that's *half* the time. That clever wittiness in your emails might slide right past your colleagues.

You're not as good at writing emails as you think you are. Heck, you're not even as good at *reading* them as you believe. Nick Morgan, author of *Can You Hear Me*, found that people interpreted a simple two-line message of "Nice work" or "Great job" as being sarcastic 60 percent of the time.

Getting the tone right is a serious challenge in business emails, whether you're creating a marketing email in a specific brand voice or tackling a delicate topic with a colleague. If you know that the subject is particularly sensitive or important, take extra care. (See chapter #28, "Writing the Tough Email.") Even ordinary, transactional emails can go wrong in spectacular ways, as the story of the angry author reveals.

The world of distributed work and virtual teams makes tone even more critical, since we lack the in-person interactions that give us a better grounding for interpreting intention and mood. When you collaborate in virtual teams with people you rarely see in person, you may not understand one person's dry sense of humor or the way another one talks through problems.

Even in your ordinary, everyday exchanges with people, pay attention to how you communicate the underlying tone.

Add signals of intention. Often, you can clarify your tone with a few key comments or phrases. (*I'm truly happy to hear this!*) Punctuation and emojis can point the reader in the right direction. Exclamation points can stand in for cheerful excitement, while a winking or smiling emoji indicates an attempt at humor.

Consider your history with the recipient. A friend or colleague who knows you well will generally interpret your tone by filling in what they know of your personality and speaking or writing style.

If you are breaking out of your normal patterns, you'll need to work harder to communicate tone. For example, if you take pride in being the office grouch and try to write a supportive or witty message, the recipient is likely to read it as grumpy. In that case, be explicit: *I am genuinely excited about this news— no snarkiness intended.*

Avoid sarcasm. Sarcasm almost never works in email. It's simply too subtle for an attention-deprived medium. If you must make a sarcastic retort, flag it. [*Sarcasm alert!*]

Use humor with care. Humor depends heavily on context, and is tough to translate without timing and body language. Stripped of its context, a clever quip about a team member might read as a cruel remark. Self-deprecating humor is safer, but it can undermine your authority if used too frequently or to minimize your skills or knowledge.

Consider the context. Some situations are fraught with emotional peril, if not on your part, then the recipient's. For example, what if a new hire asks you for feedback on their project? The request may only entail a few minutes of reviewing something for you. For them, it's an important career objective. When providing feedback, you may need to take extra steps to manage the tone of the interaction. Likewise, if you're writing in a language that is not the native language for the recipient, your tone may be misconstrued.

In these situations, you can supplement the email with a voice or video recording. My son Mark introduced me to a growing trend for including links to short video clips with emails. He uses video when providing feedback for his team members, so they can hear his vocal inflections and see his face. That's a great way to make sure people understand your tone. (See AnneJanzer.com/Resources for suggested tools.)

WHAT TO DO IF YOU'RE MISINTERPRETED

Don't blame the reader. Take responsibility as the author of the email, no matter what your intentions were. Apologize, using your own words. Here's how I might do it:

> *My apologies. I intended to express support and encouragement, and clearly I failed. I will do better in the future.*

#10 PROBLEMATIC PUNCTUATION

If you're of a certain age, you may have come to email from the world of writing for print. You internalized all of those rules about when to use periods and commas. You understand that exclamation points are practically forbidden, legitimate only for dialog and extreme caution: *Danger!*

So you may shudder at the punctuation you see in emails and social media channels. Stop shuddering. It's time to learn new punctuation rules, at least for emails and other digital communications.

Punctuation marks and smiling emojis add layers of meaning that we desperately need in the virtual world. In emails, no one can see the twinkle in our eyes when we make a joke, or hear the clever way we time our delivery. They have only the words. And they approach them from whatever mood they're in.

New rules of punctuation have emerged from texting and instant messaging, where tight character limits and thumb-based typing have inspired creative solutions for communicating quickly and clearly. The adjustments evolved into a *de facto* language of tone using punctuation and emojis, as well as terms and abbreviations (*OMG*). Generations who have grown up texting and messaging bring this language with them as they adopt email in the business world.

DON'T CLING TO PRINT-BASED PUNCTUATION RULES

Punctuation rules for texting and social media messaging differ from those for print communications.

Emails inhabit that nebulous zone in between print and texting or social media. Sometimes they are formal, sometimes they are breezy and friendly. If you insist rigidly on proper, print-based punctuation in your emails, you may confuse or offend people. That's right, you need separate punctuation rules for different media. Let's look at the key players.

EXCLAMATION POINTS

 "The return of the exclamation point is one of the most epic comebacks in punctuation history—and it's a cautionary tale for those of us who don't intuitively keep up with the times." – Erica Dhawan, *Digital Body Language*

In printed text, exclamation points are generally like spicy peppers—a little goes a long way. You've probably been taught to use them sparingly. Many copyeditors will strike them from nonfiction manuscripts.

In texting and messaging, exclamation points convey excitement, support, and encouragement. According to Erica Dhawan, a consultant and speaker on teamwork and collaboration and author of *Digital Body Language*, women often use them because "the exclamation point serves as a text-based version of the nods, smiles, and laughs that typically suffuse female friendships."

More than half (53 percent) of my LinkedIn network who responded to a survey said they use exclamation points often to show excitement or support. A fifth said they almost *never* use them. And many people said they use them in texts, but not emails.

If you enjoy exclamation points, particularly in less-formal emails, go ahead and use them within reason. Pamela Wilson, an email marketing wiz and author of several books on content marketing, allows herself one per email. That's not a bad rule. And if you see them in emails you receive, don't judge the sender's schooling. That person may be following the new rules, not the old ones.

PERIODS

It used to be so simple: put a period at the end of a sentence. Period. But again, the medium matters. For digital natives, a period at the end of a text message can indicate anger.

Imagine getting this text from your spouse: *Come home now.*

Ouch, that does sound angry, or at least it would make you think.

Of course, if you typically write long, grammatically correct sentences, no one will interpret a period as anger. But beware of sending a one-line email that looks like it could have been a text message, with just a single period. *Let's talk tomorrow.*

Even if your intentions were benign, the recipient may not sleep well worrying about what it means. If exclamation points indicate friendliness toward that person, their absence may indicate the opposite.

Periods can also be used to mimic speech in a fun way. *Best. Dog. Ever.*

That's fun, informal, and okay. Even in books.

ELLIPSES...

I went through an ellipsis phase several years ago. They can be fun for the writer because they let us off the hook for completing our sentences. They add an air of mystery.

However, that mystery or ambiguity might irritate the reader. If you love using ellipses in your writing, reconsider it, at least in business emails. Tone is too important to leave hanging.

ALL CAPS

I struggle to think of situations where all capitalization works well in emails, except in trademarked names or acronyms. All caps generally appear either shouty/angry or oblivious (WHERE IS THE CAPS LOCK KEY?), neither of which is good for your personal or professional appearance. Bold text is a better way to add emphasis, and even that should be used sparingly.

HOW FORMAL DO YOU NEED TO BE?

Before you adopt new, looser rules of punctuation, first consider the context. How formal is the recipient? Are there cultural differences? Corporate differences?

If you don't know a person well and you are communicating formally, stick to the usual print rules. Let the words express your tone. If you're excited about an opportunity, you can simply write: *I'm excited about this opportunity.*

#11 EMOJI MISFIRES

I never thought I'd say this, but yes, it's okay to use emojis in work-related emails—but with restraint, and depending on the context of the message. Otherwise, those smiley faces might cause frowns.

EMOJIS = INFORMAL

Given their origins in the world of texting, emojis automatically tip the message to an informal tone. That's one of their key benefits: they convey a sense of fun or lightness.

But they're not a "get out of jail free" card for tone. If you criticize a colleague in a message to your team, putting a smiley face on it won't help.

Emojis contribute to or clarify tone, but they cannot reverse it.

DON'T MAKE THEM STAND ALONE

Emojis can be difficult to distinguish, especially if you're using less-common ones or if the recipient isn't familiar with them. (*Why is that face blue?*) They can also be hard to make out on small screens. (*What animal is that?*) Make sure they supplement rather than replace the text.

DON'T OVERLOAD THE EMOJIS

A string of emojis is fun in a text message to a friend. It's probably too informal for most work emails.

Worse, you may alienate people. Any vision-impaired recipients may use text-to-speech software that describes each emoji. That could be fine for one or two images, but no one wants to listen to a string of descriptions: *hands pressed together, smiling face with sunglasses, birthday cake.* That wastes the recipient's time.

BEWARE OF CULTURAL DIFFERENCES

Hand gestures have varying meanings in different cultures. If you're emailing people in other countries or your team includes people newly arrived from other places, avoid most of the gesture-related options.

TRY STAGE DIRECTIONS

If there isn't a perfect match for your concept, consider creating a "verbal" emoji, written as a stage direction:

[*wink, wink*]
[*Collapses exhausted in a heap*]

EMOJI PUNCTUATION RULES

While I gathered suggestions for this book, a friend asked, "Does the emoji come before or after the punctuation?" Gosh, I love writers who try to follow the rules even as the rules are evolving!

According to the general consensus, if the emoji comes at the end of a sentence, put it *after* the end punctuation and include a space before the emoji.

#12 THE UNWELCOMING WALL OF WORDS

Look at your email before you send it. How densely do the words populate the screen? How long are the sentences that people will need to navigate? Your recipient(s) may read your message on a tiny phone screen while distracted by life around them, or on an obligatory "email inbox sweep" before getting back to the important work they are paid to do.

On a small screen, your carefully crafted paragraphs may look like a solid wall of words, massive and intimidating. Readers may decide to read the message later, when they have more time. Some never return.

And what about the colleague with a different native language? That person might need to translate that massive block of words before they can respond. That's asking a lot.

Don't scare the reader off with a giant wall of words. For online reading, shorten the sentences and break up the paragraphs.

SHORTER SENTENCES

Be considerate to the distracted brain reading your email, and pack fewer critical ideas into each sentence. You are also less likely to make grammatical errors in shorter sentences, so everyone wins.

Look for sentences with independent clauses (parts that could stand on their own) and make them into multiple sentences if it makes sense.

Hemingway wrote in short sentences. You can too.

ELIMINATE UNNECESSARY WORDS

Once you've written the draft, look for words that don't contribute meaning. Here are a few likely candidates:

- *Really, very, some, kind of*: These words tend to weaken your prose
- *In order to* can almost always become "to"
- *In fact, Honestly, As it turns out*: These filler phrases can usually go without being missed

SHORTER PARAGRAPHS

On a small screen, even a few sentences can add up to an imposing, solid paragraph. If you want people to act on or internalize your email quickly, break up those long paragraphs into shorter ones. Put the points you most want to emphasize in their own paragraphs.

A single-sentence paragraph makes a bigger impact.

THE COFFEE TEST

Don't know if your email is too dense? Here's a fun test: send the email to yourself, then read it on your phone while waiting in line for coffee or making yourself a cup of tea. You may be surprised.

#13 WASTED SUBJECT LINES

An email subject line must accomplish two important tasks.

1. **Inspire opening**: The subject line should identify what the message is about, so people can decide when and where to read it.
2. **Aid retrieval**: The subject line helps people sort and categorize messages they don't act on immediately.

If you want to be effective communicating through email, write subject lines that accomplish both of those goals. Yes, it takes thought and care. You might want to write the subject line last, after completing the body of the message.

Most of us don't think enough about the subject lines of the emails we send. Too often, we focus on only the first goal, getting the recipient to open the email. Sometimes we don't even manage that.

FIVE COMMON FAILURES

Here are five ways work-related email subjects can, and do, fail.

1. Meaningless subjects. *Email. Hello. A message for you.* These content-free subject lines fail on both objectives, opening and retrieval. Use them, and you'll reduce the odds that the recipient reads your message.

2. Too much in the subject line. Short subjects are good. Email systems truncate long subject lines and add text like [FWD] when forwarding.

Some people put the whole message in the subject line, then leave the body empty. I've also seen emails where the subject line starts a sentence and the message body concludes it. Either approach violates our expectations.

3. Emoji-laden subject lines. One or two emojis might communicate tone or catch the reader's attention. But not everyone can see them easily on small screens. Vision-impaired people must listen to software describe each image. And if you pile on too many, your emails may start to look spammy or unprofessional.

4. The clickbait subject line. Email marketers spend hours polishing and testing lines that entice people to open the email: *Exciting opportunity! I can't believe I did this!* These curiosity-inducing headlines are designed to increase open rates, without regard for an ongoing relationship. Avoid them. You might entice someone to click but won't help them find the email later.

5. Spammy-sounding subject lines. You might inadvertently catch the attention of spam filters by using words like *Free, Please read,* and *sale* in your subject lines.

Those five practices are what *not* to do. Now let's look at *effective* subject lines.

SUMMARIZE THE EMAIL

A successful subject line lets the recipient know what to expect in the message, so they can decide how carefully, and when, to read it. Even better, can your subject line do either of the following?

- Communicate urgency, or lack thereof
- Broadcast the tone of the message: is this a formal request? A funny commentary?

If you're not sure how to summarize the content, revisit chapter #1, on unnecessary emails. What's your reason for sending this message, and why should the recipient read it? Clear, direct subject lines work well:

Background for our interview Monday
Progress: On track for September 15 launch
Can you approve this quote by Friday?

Clarity is more important than cleverness.

If it's not urgent, let people know. FYI (For Your Information) is a useful abbreviation for tagging informational updates.

WRITE SEARCHABLE SUBJECTS

What are the chances your recipient is going to act on your email immediately when they first see it? Slim. So, they'll need to retrieve it. If an email involves multiple recipients and turns into a conversation, it will stick around for a while. People will want to return to it.

Many people use email like a giant filing cabinet for

communications. Conversations in messages with meaningless subject lines are like misfiled documents—hard to find.

How would you want to retrieve this email in the future? Write a subject line that helps your future self as well as others. If the email is transactional, completing a step in a process, indicate that in the title: *Completed Acme contract.*

SIMPLE STRATEGIES FOR TEAMS

When you communicate regularly with the same group of people, you can agree on acronyms to streamline your email handling. Acronyms make better use of that short subject line.

Sarah Tetlow, CEO of Firm Focus and an email productivity coach, advises teams to agree on using a few simple acronyms in subject lines:

AR – Action Required
NAR – No Action Required

Erica Dhawan, author of *Digital Body Language*, suggests a few others:

WINFY – What I Need From You
ROM – Reply on Monday (useful for emails sent on weekends)

#14 LOSING FACE WITH CUT AND PASTE

If you frequently do similar tasks over email, reusing messages or message templates saves time and energy. Email consultant Sarah Tetlow, creator of the ARTT email productivity system, suggests that people create an email folder of templates for messages they write repeatedly. While you can also cut and paste from previous messages, assembling frequently used emails in one folder makes locating them easier.

Of course, you'll get better results if you personalize the email. No one likes form letters. And herein lies the danger.

My friend Marti Konstant, a workplace futurist and author of *Activate Your Agile Career*, shared her story of cut and paste gone wrong: she forgot to change the recipient's name before she hit *Send*. As Marti said, "There is almost no way to walk this back. Apologizing for it seems to make it worse."

Hiring managers report getting emails from prospective candidates thanking them for the interview, but with the wrong company name. These accidents make it clear to the recipient that you're cutting and pasting. There's no shame in it, really. The shame lies in not checking carefully.

Go ahead and use templates, but give yourself a safety net using the practices below.

WORK FROM A TEMPLATE RATHER THAN A PREVIOUS EMAIL

If you regularly send similar emails to multiple people, take the extra step of making a generic email template with clearly marked areas to complete. Put the variable sections in all capital letters, making it clear which sections you will need to work on.

For example:

Hello NAME,
ADD PERSONAL CONNECTION PARAGRAPH.
Would you be interested in reading my latest book? It's all about writing effective business emails, and might be useful for your DEPARTMENT team at COMPANY NAME.

There's *almost* no way you're going to miss the parts that need personalizing. Although, occasionally I have received an email with [YOUR NAME HERE] fields left in them. They are always entertaining.

If you use templates, leave the *To* field blank until you're finished. This eliminates the risk of sending the template. Always check the entire message carefully if you're copying and pasting from another email or template.

BEWARE OF SUBTLE FORMATTING CLUES AND GLITCHES

When you copy from a program like Microsoft Word into an email client, the text often brings HTML-based formatting tags along with it. You may not notice that formatting in your email client, but your recipient will see font changes.

This looks confusing and messy, and gives away the fact that you have pasted the content from another source.

There's a quick fix. When copying text into an email, paste the text without its formatting, so it matches the rest of the content.

- On a Mac, you can usually find *Paste and Match Style* in an Edit menu, or use *Option + Command + Shift +V*
- On a PC, the *Ctrl + Shift + V* sequence should do the trick.

The final test, of course, is to email the message to yourself and make sure the formatting looks right before sending it to the recipient.

#15 OVERDOING FONTS AND FORMATS

The advent of desktop publishing in the mid-1980s marked a pivotal moment when print layout stopped belonging exclusively to design experts. All you needed was a desktop computer and relatively friendly software like PageMaker to format nearly anything. And boy, did people format! The world was suddenly flooded with newsletters, brochures, fliers, and more created by eager novices.

Drunk with the new powers at their fingertips, people deployed *all* of the features available to them: columns, bold and italicized text, multiple typefaces, and varying point sizes. A few abandoned the conventions of print design completely for flashing fonts.

What software engineer thought flashing text would be a good idea?

Eventually, most people learned restraint. But we see echoes of that time when a colleague discovers the HTML formatting capabilities in their email client, a generous menu that may include:

- A variety of font families
- Bold, italics, underline, and strikethrough
- Text colors
- Colored highlighting
- Indentation and alignment
- Bulleted and numbered lists

As you face this mouthwatering menu of possibilities, remember the following two rules:

1. Use formatting to aid the reader's comprehension or guide their attention.
2. Never let formatting distract from the message itself.

Here are a few guidelines to help you live with those principles.

STICK WITH ONE FORM OF EMPHASIS

Formatting can help you catch the reader's attention or emphasize the most important part of the message, such as a deadline or call to action. Bold works well for this. Or italics. Or colored highlighting. But not all of them.

Pick one design element to use for emphasis and then stick with it. If you use highlighting in one place and italics elsewhere, your message will look messy and confusing.

HELP THE SCANNERS AND MULTI-PASS READERS

If your email covers several subjects, you can break it into sections with bold subheadings. Subheads help people find what they need when they revisit the messages later.

USE LISTS

For long messages, consider using either bulleted or numbered lists. This formatting option makes it easier for the scanning reader to see that you have multiple points.

And yes, it makes a difference which one you choose.

Use numbers when you *need* numbers:

- When the order matters (#1 needs to happen before #2)
- When you want people to draw attention to how many there are (*I have three questions for you.*)
- When you want to refer back to entries on the list (*I have a question about item #2.*)

Otherwise, use bullets. Numbers add a bit of complexity that detracts from your meaning.

If you have a long list of points to communicate, consider breaking it up into multiple messages. That may be a better option if you need action or responses on each point.

DON'T FORGET ABOUT WHITE SPACE

Designers, artists, and musicians understand the importance of *negative space*. It's the silence between the notes in music, or the margins of a paper manuscript. The white space guides our attention.

Add white space to your email by keeping paragraphs short and separating ideas with blank lines.

STICK TO ONE OR TWO ORDINARY FONTS

It's okay to use a different font for subheadings than the body of the message. But otherwise, stick to the default font provided or stay on the boring, safe side. The font you find fun and quirky may annoy others. (Comic Sans is a great example. You can really irritate a designer by sending them an email using Comic Sans.)

USE COLOR SPARINGLY

A single highlighted sentence or colored phrase will pop. Multiple colors may look disorganized and busy. They may not show up the same way on every email client, so make sure that the email still makes sense in black and white.

CHECK THE FORMATTING BY SENDING IT TO YOURSELF

The software someone uses to read your email (the email client) can affect the way it looks. Some people may turn off images. Others may not display the formatting you expect. Especially if you are sending email outside your organization, you cannot count on it coming across exactly as planned.

Mail your nicely formatted message to yourself and read it on a different device. If you composed it on your desktop, read it on your phone, or vice versa. Does the formatting work? Simplest is safest.

#16 FUMBLING THE SIGN-OFF

You've thought about the purpose, put care into crafting the message. Now, how do you wrap things up? *Regards? Best wishes?* Just your name? Each alternative has fans and detractors.

By the time you're done composing the email message, you don't want to spend more brain cycles closing it out. Yet the sign-off deserves a moment of thought, especially for important emails or messages to people you don't know well.

The sign-off serves many purposes:

- It lets the reader know they've reached the end. They know that the email message hasn't been cut off and there's nothing more to scroll through.
- It contributes to an overall sense of politeness and may signal the nature of your relationship. Do you take the time to thank the recipient and wish them well? Do you end with *Your friend* or *Best wishes?*
- The sign-off can also reinforce the content or remind the recipient of what you are requesting.

Here are a few approaches for ending emails.

CLOSE THE DOOR GENTLY AS YOU LEAVE

For a longer, formal email, a short wrap-up at the end helps the recipient understand that they've finished the meat of the message. Ending without a sign-off is the virtual equivalent of leaving the room abruptly when you're done with business.

If the message is long and packed with information, consider thanking the recipient or letting them know that you're open to questions: *Thanks for reading this long and detailed message. Please let me know if anything isn't clear.*

The end is a great place to subtly remind the recipient of what you need from them. *I look forward to seeing your feedback.*

THE CLOSING SALUTATION

The usual, safe options work well for formal emails:

Best,
Best wishes,
Regards,
Warm regards,
Sincerely,
Yours,

People have strong opinions about these. I feel that if someone is offended by a choice of sign-off phrase, they are spending too much energy taking offense. Pick one that feels comfortable and use it regularly.

Save *Love* for family emails rather than work. I know people say that work is like family, but let's not take that too far.

If the message is informal and you know your recipient well, you can use the sign-off to infuse humor related to the text of the email.

CLOSING WITH YOUR NAME ONLY

Ending with just your name is quick and shows the recipient that you've reached the end. I do this often, but in certain situations it might appear too informal or abrupt.

If you're moving quickly and are familiar with the other person, you can use initials. Be aware, though, that while a single initial can appear friendly, it can also feel abrupt or cold. Tone is tricky.

THE SHRINKING SIGN-OFF

If you're in the middle of an ongoing, back-and-forth email exchange, the sign-offs often get progressively shorter. At a certain point you might dispense with the sign-off altogether. If this happens all the time, it's worth asking: is there a better way to have these conversations?

UNSURE?

Don't waste too many precious mental cycles agonizing over how to close your emails. Pick a couple of standard approaches for more formal emails, and use your name for less formal ones. For someone new or from a different culture, consider mirroring what they do.

TIMESAVING TIP

If you write the same sign-off constantly, save yourself time and put it in your signature block. Turn the page for more details.

#17 NEGLECTING THE SIGNATURE

Who the heck is this?

Ever get an email from someone you didn't know well and try to figure it out from the context? Chances are you scrolled to the bottom for the automated bit of text at the end: the email signature or signature block.

Automated signatures add structure and context to your emails. You can fill them with your full name, title, phone number, website, or any follow-up information you want to share. Best of all, it happens without you thinking about it.

The email signature takes the pressure off the sign-off. You don't have to worry about whether to include your full name if it's automatically added to the end of your messages. This is a great place to add subtle context, especially if you are communicating with a new correspondent. You might include a one-liner about what you do.

Things you might put in your signature block include:

- Your title, especially if you work in a large organization

- Your phone number or other communication channels you choose to share
- Your website/blog/books/social media: wherever you'd send people to find out more about you
- How to pronounce your name, especially if it's a tricky one. Spell it out phonetically, give a rhyming word, or include a link to a recording.
- The pronouns you prefer people to use for you (she/her, they/them, etc.). Karen Catlin, author of *Better Allies*, suggests using the email signature to normalize the practice of sharing pronouns.
- Expectations for responsiveness. If you send emails at odd hours (early mornings, late evenings), let people know you don't expect the same from them.

You can also set up signatures for specific devices, like the familiar phone-related disclaimer: *Sent from my mobile device, excuse the brevity.*

If you always end your emails in the same way, you could add the sign-off to your signature block.

PRO TIP: USE MULTIPLE SIGNATURES

Most mail clients let you set up multiple email signatures and pick from them depending on the situation.

You could set a default signature with your contact information, and another with a meeting scheduling link that you only add when a message might spark a follow-up meeting. You can also use this to subtly inform the recipient of a new project without explicitly mentioning it.

#18 ATTACHMENT ISSUES

Many of the email horror stories people send me are related to attachments. It's possible to mess up this simple task in ways that damage your reputation. Let's take a tour of the problems, and how to avoid them.

THE MYSTERY ATTACHMENT

A friend shared the story of an email she once received that had the subject "Email." The body of the message read "Please see attached." And the attachment was titled "Document 1."

Wow, that message really sold the attached document!

Even if the email's primary task is to serve as an envelope for the document, it should achieve two things:

1. Getting the recipient's attention to open the message
2. Setting the context for the attachment (why are you sending this thing and why should they open it?)

People are wary of opening attachments from people they don't know well, for security reasons. (*Is this malware?*) Make sure they understand what the attachment is and why they're getting it. And if the recipient is going to file or keep the document, give it a meaningful name.

THE FORGOTTEN ATTACHMENT

Have you ever forgotten to attach a document? You carefully craft a message about a proposal or report or invoice, and spend so much time describing the attachment and fussing over the message that you forget to attach the file.

Come on. I know I'm not the only one who does this.

If you catch it right away, you can fire off a second email with the attachment and a quick apology or joke. That's only mildly embarrassing. But if you don't notice it yourself, the recipient has to reply to ask for the attachment. Now you've wasted everyone's time.

Worse, and potentially more embarrassing, is attaching the wrong file. My favorite story in this vein is about the job applicant who attached a photo of the actor Nicolas Cage instead of his résumé when applying.

What do you do if you forget an attachment or send the wrong one?

First, don't kick yourself. You are not alone. Most of us have done the same thing. Just don't become known as the person who always messes up attachments.

Correct the problem with good humor. Humor directed at yourself is nearly always safe. There's research to show that when people make a mistake that is unrelated to their area of expertise, we tend to like them better. The name for this is the *Pratfall Effect*.

HELP FOR ATTACHMENT ISSUES

Google Mail occasionally nudges me when I hit *Send*. It displays a message like this:

> It seems like you forgot to attach a file. You wrote "I've attached" in your message, but there are no files attached. Send anyway?

That message has saved me a few times. Most versions of Microsoft Outlook have a similar feature, the Forgotten Attachment Reminder.

But don't count on software to rescue you. For example, Google does not detect a missing attachment if I use less obvious wording, such as "You'll find a copy of the proposal included with this email."

If you catch it right away, you may be able to "Undo" sending the email. See chapter #25, "Sending Without a Safety Net."

The surest solution is changing your habits. As soon as you find yourself typing the word "attached," stop instantly and attach the file. This is one more thing to check for when you give the email a once-over before sending.

19 SELF-ABSORBED OPENINGS

After the email subject, the opening sentences do the most important work of the message. The first words show up in email previews, and a few people may never read further.

An effective opening gets to the point of the message. But it must also catch the reader's attention and inspire them to read on. You'll have a better chance of getting their attention if you make the first sentence all about them.

What's our favorite topic? *Ourselves*. It's the one we know best. Hence, when we write an email, it tends to be all about us, the writer. As we compose the message, we think about our own needs and motivations and send messages filled with *I*, *me*, and *my*.

Your recipient, however, has their own needs and viewpoints. Bring them into the picture from the start to break through the clutter of words demanding their attention.

For example, you may automatically open an email like this: *I have a quick question about ...*

That's a fine start, but this might be better: *Do you know the answer to this question...*

If you want to notify your correspondent of a schedule change, lead with *their* needs, not yours.

Change this: *I just found out that the project is delayed.*

To this: *You should know that the project date has slipped.*

A meeting request, likewise, should be direct.

Instead of this: *I've scheduled a meeting for 1pm Tuesday.*

Try this: *Please come to the meeting on Tuesday, at 1pm.*

You get the idea.

There's still room in emails for politeness. If you're writing to a stranger, introduce yourself first. Find a common connection if you can: *We both belong to the Central Coast Writer's group. I'm an author working on ...*

This focus on the reader doesn't have to stop at the introduction. Look over your message and see how many sentences you can reframe from the reader's perspective, while still being polite and not demanding. This simple change alone will make your emails much more effective, and may strengthen your relationship.

You may not remember to do this as you draft an email. I often forget. But you can make a quick revision before pressing *Send.*

#20 EMAILS NEVER DIE (AND AREN'T PRIVATE)

You see an email, you fire off an answer and move on with your day. It's all in the past now, right?

Not exactly.

An email may seem impermanent, fleeting, and private. But it long outlasts the attention you pay to it, and could haunt you later. Check what you're saying before you send messages to other people's mailboxes and corporate email servers.

Once you send an email, you lose control over what others do with your words. They might forward the message to people you never intended to see it.

Years ago, my friend Stephan emailed his boss a response to a customer question. He included a funny quip directed to his boss, not the customer. He assumed his boss would extract the answer from his email to send to the customer. Did that happen? No. He forwarded the email verbatim, complete with inside joke.

I find *two* important lessons in that story. First, never assume people will read your emails thoroughly. Second, never forward an email without reading it.

Emails can end up visible to other people in many ways. Your recipient might leave your message open on their laptop in a public place or read it in a meeting with others nearby. They might print it out on a printer where others can read it. It's out of your control.

EMPLOYERS CAN READ YOUR EMAILS

Employers can monitor emails on corporate servers. If you and the recipient work for different entities and are using corporate email servers, the email you send will live on in both places.

Even after you delete messages, they live in backups and email archives. That fact has caught up with many people over the years, often to their surprise.

PART OF A "PERMANENT RECORD"

Without giving legal advice, I can safely say that emails can have legal ramifications:

- Courts have considered agreements made over email to be legally binding contracts.
- Law enforcement authorities can seize emails, although they may need a warrant.
- Emails may be part of the legal discovery process, gathering information related to litigation.

If you dream of using your company's growing market dominance to squelch the competition, for heaven's sake, don't elaborate on those thoughts in an email to your executive team. Mark Zuckerberg's emails about Instagram have been presented in Congressional subcommittee hearings and a Supreme Court case.

Don't *do* anything illegal or ethically questionable at work, and if your discussions could be construed as questionable, don't send them in email.

If you have any concerns about privacy, don't use email.

#21 UNDERMINING YOUR AUTHORITY

A director-level employee in a fast-growing tech start-up got puzzling feedback that her emails weren't "good." She had no problem communicating in person with her team, colleagues, and management. She reached out to me.

When I looked at a few sample email chains, the problem jumped right out. Informal conversational patterns were slipping into the written emails. When I read the emails literally, it sounded like she was unwilling to take a stance or not confident in her opinions.

Her emails were undermining her.

Many conversational language patterns fall flat in print. Indirect speech is one of them.

INDIRECT SPEECH PATTERNS

Robin Lakoff, a professor of linguistics at the University of California, Berkeley, who studies language and gender, describes four patterns of *tentative speech*.

1. Expressions of uncertainty: *I think, perhaps,* or disclaimers like *I may be mistaken.*
2. Hedges: Weakening words and phrases like *sort of, kind of,* or *somewhat*
3. Tag questions: Phrases or questions seeking immediate confirmation (*Isn't it? Don't you agree?*)
4. Intensifiers: Words like *really* or *very* that, despite appearances, weaken rather than strengthen the point. (I'm *really* serious.)

These patterns crop up all the time in our speech. For those of us who try to write as we speak, they also appear in the first draft of our writing.

According to Deborah Tannen, a professor of linguistics at Georgetown University and prolific author who studies how men and women communicate, we use indirect speech patterns to build and manage relationships:

- Leveling the playing field when communicating with someone with less authority than ourselves, making a request sound like less of a demand
- Inviting collaboration and contributions from others (*What do you think?*)
- Expressing politeness or courtesy

Men and women use these speech patterns. But women who use them in a work environment face a greater risk of being seen as unsure of themselves.

Our speaking styles often leak into our written words. If you're writing a quick email to a colleague, typing as you think, you are likely to fall into your usual conversational rituals. And that instinct can damage you. People tend to interpret written material literally, even if they know you well.

If you open a message with *This might be a stupid question,* the reader could infer that you don't know your facts, or don't have a strong opinion of your capabilities. Even if you know the recipient well and speak frequently, remember that the recipient may forward it to others who lack that background.

Your words represent you when you are not present. Make sure they project the image you want them to.

ELIMINATE SIGNS OF UNCERTAINTY

The solution to this problem is simple: look for and remove markers of tentative speech when they show up in your business writing, including emails.

Weed out the weakening words. Remove common intensifiers by searching for words like *very, really,* and *quite* that promise to make the meaning stronger but often weaken it.

Trim the hedges. Look for waffling words like *some, sort of, just,* and *kind of.* My personal nemesis is *a bit,* which stubbornly creeps into my first drafts.

Distinguish the real unknowns from conversational hedges. You may need qualifying words to express the true unknowns, particularly if you're writing about technical or academic subjects. If the hedge words increase accuracy, keep them. Be clear about it. And consider clarifying your certainty or uncertainty.

I'm 80 percent confident that this will happen.

Maintain the right amount of politeness. If you worry about the tone sounding impolite or too abrupt, leave in one or two flourishes and delete the rest. But when you want to appear professional, confident, and authoritative, don't put qualifiers or hedges around your expertise. Be uncertain about the weather, but certain about your facts.

#22 MISTAKES YOU SHOULD HAVE CAUGHT

Before you send the message, look carefully at what you've written.

This may be the single most important practice in this book. It sounds so simple, yet in our rush to be more productive, we often neglect a final check. And that neglect can backfire spectacularly.

In researching this book, I asked people on my Writing Practices email list about their email failures. They responded with stories of sending messages to the wrong recipients, leaving text from a previous copy in the email, finding embarrassing typos, and worse. One told me about the time her phone helpfully changed a request for *torque* tools to *torture* tools. I hope her team had a good laugh.

Entertaining as they are, most of these blunders could have been prevented by taking a moment to read the email first.

SOFTWARE HELPS, BUT NOT ENOUGH

There's almost no excuse to send an email with an obvious spelling or grammar error. Most email clients include basic spelling and grammar checking, and you can add third-party tools for more help. (See the resources on AnneJanzer.com for suggestions.)

If you don't have grammar and spelling tools available in your email client, consider writing first drafts elsewhere and then pasting the text into the mail message.

But software cannot check everything. It cannot detect when you've spelled a word correctly but used the wrong word altogether. For example, you might use the word *break* instead of *brake*, and it will fly right past spelling checkers. And they cannot spot when you may be communicating the wrong tone. For that, you need the human touch.

CHECK BEFORE YOU SEND: THE ONCE-OVER

If you do nothing else, read through the email once slowly, including the subject line. Typos in subject lines are extra embarrassing. Is there anything you'd change or that the reader might misinterpret? Do you have too many five-syllable words? Are you including jargon that the recipient might not know?

GIVE IT THE GPS TEST

The acid test for most writing is reading it aloud. When you force yourself to do this, you are more likely to catch wording or punctuation problems. If *you* trip over your words, anyone skimming the email will likely do the same.

To test for tone and clarity, read it aloud in a monotone voice. Think of the automated navigation voice on a GPS system. It doesn't use inflection to convey urgency or meaning. It's placid and even: *In fifty feet, turn right on Main Street.*

Does your email make sense when stripped of all vocal inflection? If you find yourself wanting to emphasize words to clarify what you mean, you may be misleading the reader.

If sections of your message fail the GPS test, consider breaking them down into smaller, simpler sentences with less room for going astray.

MAIL IT TO YOURSELF

If you really want to test how an email will land, mail it to yourself first. Open it on a different kind of device: if you wrote it on a laptop, open it on a phone or tablet.

How does the email subject line look in your inbox?

Changing devices helps you see the text with fresh eyes, providing some distance from what you thought you were saying. You are more likely to spot issues with clarity, subject lines, formatting, and tone.

QUICK FIX: THE SAFETY BRAKE

Put on a safety brake by keeping the *To* field empty until you've reviewed the email.

My friend MB Deans puts it this way: "When composing a new email, *never* address it to anyone until you're 110% sure you want to send it. That way, if you hit *Send* reflexively, your email will throw up a warning, and you have one more chance for review. I can't tell you how many times this has saved my bacon."

When you feel good about the body of the message and the subject line, replace the *To* field and double-check the recipients.

#23 THE WRONG RECIPIENTS

Many of the worst email disasters involve sending things to the wrong people. Here are a couple of representative stories from my network:

- One of my LinkedIn connections (who shall remain nameless here) was a new employee at a large, international software company. He forwarded a mildly inappropriate joke to a friend at work, but made a typo in his friend's email address, which caused it to change to the address for a corporate-wide distribution list. His off-color joke was cued up to go to thousands of people around the globe. Happily, the email list automatically rejected the message, or his tenure at that company would have been short.
- One friend complained about a colleague in an email to his manager, then accidentally sent the message to the colleague instead of the manager.

Save yourself from these situations. Even if you don't want to take the time to reread the content of your emails before sending them, *always* check the *To* field, whether you are originating the email chain or replying to one.

BEWARE OF AUTO-COMPLETE AND SUGGESTED RECIPIENTS

Do you actually remember anyone's email address? Or do you count on your email software to offer the right option when you start typing a name?

I'm definitely in that latter camp. Sometimes I don't even remember a person's last name. So I type the first name, the mailer shows a menu, and *presto*—an email accident waiting to happen. Ironically, I once picked the wrong "Anne" from a list of correspondents when sending a message to a client.

Always check those automatically populated email addresses.

In addition to completing an email address from the start, software sometimes recommends that you *add* an address to a chain in the *cc* field, based on previous mailing patterns. If you regularly communicate with three other people as a group, it might prompt you to add the third on a message to the other two. It's easy to accept that suggestion without noticing. And that can be awkward if the point of the email was to complain about the third person.

OUT-OF-CONTROL *CC*S

Fun fact: The "cc" on the *cc* field stands for *carbon copy*, a throwback to when typists used carbon paper to make duplicates of letters or forms. In the old days, you would give someone a carbon copy of a letter to read or file.

Things have changed. In large organizations, people pepper the *cc* fields with email addresses for all kinds of reasons, often not directly related to the subject of the message: showing their management how busy they are, covering their bases for potential problems, and so on. Email senders may also ask for responses from people in the *cc* field.

No wonder the email environment is so confusing.

Don't overload the *cc* field. Make sure everyone knows what you need from them. You can be explicit about what you expect: *I'm copying Sam so she'll know how close we are to completing this phase and needing her input for the next step.*

HOW AND WHY TO USE *BCC*

The *bcc* field (originally *blind carbon copy*) sends a copy of an email to an email address without it appearing on the recipient's email. The *bcc* recipient remains invisible to the people listed in the *To* or *cc* fields.

While that sounds sneaky and stealthy, it has legitimate uses and protects people's inboxes. You can give someone a glimpse into one side of an email conversation without including them in the follow-up responses. People in the *bcc* field won't see the replies that people send to you if they hit *Reply All*.

The *bcc* field does *not* propagate when someone replies to the message, so your recipient needn't worry about their response going to someone who was a *bcc* on the original message. That's a common misconception, but *bcc* doesn't work that way.

If you're sending an email to a disparate group of people and want to protect the privacy of their email addresses, send it to yourself and include everyone else in the *bcc* field.

#24 "REPLY ALL" ACCIDENTS

Reply All is, at its heart, a great time-saver. You don't have to copy and paste all of those email addresses. The software developers who first came up with this option surely thought they were doing a service to humankind.

But like most technologies, it has unintended consequences. The *Reply All* feature generates a huge amount of inbox clutter. (*Why was I included in this chain? How can I escape?*) And it's responsible for a large number of email failures.

Reply All tempts us to send messages without really noticing where they go. People you don't expect may be lurking in the *cc* field. It's easy to write a reply addressing only the sender, without realizing that your response is broadcast to a larger group.

Happily, you can protect yourself from these downsides. If you always check the recipients (as suggested in the last chapter), you will automatically spot when you've hit a problem.

QUICK FIX: CHANGE YOUR DEFAULT

Most email clients let you choose a default setting for reply: Reply or Reply All.

For example, in Google Mail, you can have the software default to:

- Reply
- Reply All
- Prompt you every time you press *Reply*

Microsoft Outlook has similar options. Never choose *Reply All* as your default. It's much easier to realize that you should have included someone than to try to "take back" an email.

If Reply All is your default setting, put the book down and change this right now. If you need help with this, ask your email administrator. You'll never have to share a *Reply All* failure story.

SAVING OTHER PEOPLE FROM REPLY ALL

If you're sending an email to a group, you can prevent others from falling into the *Reply All* trap by reminding them of the best way to reply: *Please send questions to me directly rather than the entire list.*

#25 SENDING WITHOUT A SAFETY NET

The panic hits the moment after you hit the *Send* button: *I sent it to the wrong person! I attached the wrong file! I was only halfway through writing!*

If only you could travel back in time and fix it.

Maybe you can, but only by 10 to 30 seconds or so, depending on your email client. You'll need to act quickly.

Both Gmail and Microsoft Outlook have an *Undo* feature. When you send an email, a box pops up offering the option to *Undo* for a few moments, before the email disappears for good. You can change the setting for how long that email waits in the queue before it sends.

Give yourself time to react and undo the send. I changed my default setting to 30 seconds while writing this book.

You might even be able to *recall* an unread message from the inbox of a recipient, if you are both in the same organization. (Ask your email administrator.)

There are few times in life that we can turn back the clock, even for a few seconds. This is one of them. Give yourself that safety net.

#26 NO ONE RESPONDS TO YOUR EMAILS

People aren't responding to your emails? Before you moan about how broken email is or send nagging follow-up reminders, take a good look at the emails you send.

Do you make it as easy as possible for people to know how to respond, or do you bury the request four paragraphs in? Have you provided clear and actionable instructions, and a deadline?

Everyone's email inbox is overloaded. It's your responsibility to make your important requests rise to the top, especially if you need a response to carry on with your job. This isn't simply good email etiquette. It's effective career management.

Make the extra effort when crafting messages to increase your chances of receiving a response:

Communicate your request in the subject line: With your colleagues or regular correspondents, agree on consistent labels, like "Action Required." (See chapter #13 on subject lines.) For people outside your team, consider polite variations:

Request for a review
Two things that need your input by Friday

If the email subject line identifies the message as a request, people are more likely to prioritize reading and handling it.

Open with the request. In a familiar or informal message, make the request the first item in the email, and then add the reasoning or justification.

For example:

Can you review the attached blog post by Friday?
This is part of a series we're doing for the launch, so we
need to post it on Tuesday at the latest.

Be specific and clear. Spell out exactly what you need from the recipient. You can be polite while being direct. Start with what you need, then add the reasons.

Be explicit about timing. Without a specific deadline, the recipient may kick the project to the bottom of an eternal to-do list. You can offer a deadline without being demanding:

With your response by next Friday, we can get this done
in time for the Q2 reports.

Reduce barriers and follow-up questions. Forestall additional back-and-forth messages if possible. Create a shared document that has the resources people might need, like links or examples. Include a scheduling link in the email if the subject might need a follow-up conversation.

Ask for a commitment. For major requests that cannot easily be delivered right away, ask for a commitment.

Once people make that initial commitment, they are much more likely to follow through. The wording can be simple:

Please let me know if you'll be able to do this and I'll
add you to the list.

Consider the *almost-there* reminder. Busy people procrastinate, perhaps hoping things will fall off the calendar altogether. If you haven't heard from the recipient, a gentle reminder one or two days ahead of time can make all the difference. Doing this well is a delicate balance. You don't want to sound like you're nagging.

Try framing it as an offer:

Do you need anything from me to finish the review by
Friday?

Or, disguise the reminder as an update:

FYI: We've got the graphics and social media promotion
ready and can make the schedule if you're still on course
to give us an approval by Friday.

Be patient. Your high-priority task may not be critical to the other people handling their own workloads.

Unless the project is truly urgent, give people time before you start following up. And if it's urgent, email may not be the right medium.

When you communicate with people in other countries, account for factors like time zone differences, holiday schedules, the need for consensus-building or hierarchical approvals, and time spent translating messages and replies. Also keep in mind possible cultural differences. Not every culture moves at the breakneck pace of American business. Your recipient may have a different definition of "prompt" reply.

Avoid guilt-inducing follow-ups. Do you know what drives me crazy? Cold sales emails followed by faux self-deprecating reminders meant to inspire guilt. Here's a prime example from my email inbox:

> I emailed you a short while back but didn't manage to inspire you enough to respond.

No matter what the writer's intention, it feels like an obvious attempt to make me feel guilty. This does not make me feel kindly toward the sender. Even as you construct a polite reminder email, be careful that your email can't be construed as manipulative.

And if people never reply to your emails, it's possible those messages are ending up in spam. Read on.

#27 LANDING IN SPAM

One of my first podcast interviews was on the *Marketing Book Podcast* with Douglas Burdett. It very nearly didn't happen because of a spam filter.

Several months after publishing *Subscription Marketing*, I worked up the nerve to reach out to Douglas about being a guest on his podcast. He answered, "I invited you a couple months ago, and you never responded!"

A quick search of my spam filter revealed the problem: his email had ended up there by mistake.

It all turned out well. Douglas has become a friend, and to this day he teases me about "ghosting" him. And, I adopted a new practice. About once a week, I hold my nose and take a quick look through my spam folder to see what has landed there. I've found a few gems, including:

- Foreign rights offers from international publishers
- Responses to my emails from people on my Writing Practices email list, which I *definitely* want to see
- Emails from my own family members

Spam filters are wondrous, lovely things. They protect us from a mountain of garbage and potential phishing threats. But they are imperfect. Important messages may land here by mistake. Worse, the emails *you* send to other people might land in their spam folders.

CHECK YOUR OWN FILTERS (CAREFULLY!)

Most of the time, the spam filtering technology is right on target.

That email in your folder telling you that there's money in a bank account in Nigeria? Yeah, don't open that one. A fraudster could be spoofing your friends and colleagues (pretending to send emails from them), or their accounts may have been hacked. Don't click on any attachments from the spam folder until you're certain they're legitimate. If in doubt, check with the sender: *Did you send me a link to something titled 'New Business Lead'? It's in my spam folder and I want to be certain before clicking.*

Assume the technology was right unless you're confident otherwise.

If a legitimate email ends up caught in the filter, mark it as "Not Spam" or learn how to add the sender to a list of accepted senders for your mailer.

WHEN *YOUR* EMAILS END UP IN SPAM

Any number of things can prevent your email from reaching the recipient's inbox.

Your "sender reputation." Your organization's email reputation affects whether your emails are delivered. If your company bombards people with marketing emails, people could label them as *Spam*. Spam filters learn from that behavior. When you send a message from the same domain (acme.-com, for example), the spam filters are more likely to divert it because of the corporate reputation. You may also have problems sending personal emails with a Hotmail or AOL account because these accounts have been abused in the past.

If your emails regularly land in people's spam folders, let your email administrators know about the problem.

Disguised links. Hackers and identity thieves try to get you to click on malicious links by hiding the actual destination behind a legitimate-looking cover. Spam filters look for that behavior. Although link shorteners like bitly are useful, they also disguise the destination. Including many shortened links may raise red flags.

Too many images. Spammers often try to evade text filters by sending images instead of words. So the filters are sensitive to messages containing too many images compared to the amount of text.

Spammy subjects. If you write a subject line that looks or sounds spammy, you're tempting fate. Beware of jamming subject lines with emojis, crazy punctuation, and a bunch of attention-getting words:

Free!!!!! Act now! 🎉 🍰 🧁 CAKE IN THE BREAK ROOM!!!!!!

The filters do not have a sense of humor.

Spam is a moving target. The filters are always trying to keep up with the spammers, who try to stay ahead of the filters. Look at the emails in your spam filter and avoid the tactics you see there.

#28 WRITING THE TOUGH EMAIL

Some emails are just plain hard to write. For example, the topic is sensitive. You worry that the person might misunderstand or take offense at your words. Maybe you're ending a business relationship, saying "no" to a request, or offering feedback that could be painful for the recipient to hear. Or perhaps the subject is vital to you.

People sometimes make the mistake of approaching these like any other email, or getting them out of the way quickly. You need to spend more time on them.

Here are a few tips for those emails you struggle to write.

WRITE A ROUGH DRAFT OF THE TOUGH DRAFT

First, decide whether this communication should really happen over email at all. (See chapter #33, "Emailing When There's a Better Option.") If you want or need to communicate via email, you're going to need to use nearly *all* the advice in this book. In particular, pay attention to the following practices:

Clarify your objectives before writing. What do you hope to communicate? What should the recipient do upon receiving this email? Think clearly before you type the first word.

Be alert to perceived rudeness or informality. If your words could be construed as painful or insensitive, demonstrate respect in the formalities of the email: the greeting/salutation, the sign-off, etc.

Let it sit. Ideally, draft the email the day before you plan to send it. This takes the pressure off the writing, since you know you are not actually sending it. Let it sit overnight. This gives you a better perspective. Waiting also reinforces your commitment to reviewing before you send.

REVISING BEFORE YOU SEND

When you've first composed an email, you remember exactly what you intended it to sound like in your head, so it's difficult to see how the message actually landed in the words. Use these strategies to broaden your perspective.

Send it to yourself first. As I've suggested in earlier chapters, mail the message to yourself. Then read it, ideally on another device, as if you were the recipient. You may suddenly spot potential issues.

Get an outside perspective. Run the email past a trusted friend or colleague. Meredith Fidrocki and Maura Sullivan Hill are freelance writers who work in marketing communications for education. They ask each other to do a "diplomacy check" for sensitive emails before they send them. Hill reports, "Often this leads to more collegial and productive replies."

Finally, check your own emotions. If you're upset, it will show in the message. Find more advice about that in the next chapter.

#29 EMAILING WHEN UPSET

When something or someone angers you, you may be tempted to fire off an angry missive. In the business world, as in life itself, remember the advice to count to ten. Or longer. Before sending a flaming email or irate reply, let your emotions subside so you can think clearly.

If you can, let the situation sit overnight before you respond. If the person is waiting for your response, reply with, "I've received your email, and I'll respond tomorrow." You're going to need time and thought.

WHAT DO YOU HOPE TO ACCOMPLISH?

Are you driven by the need to be right? Or do you want to be effective in moving the situation toward a better state? You may have to choose between those two options: being effective or being right. In most cases, it's best for your career to choose being effective.

What do you realistically hope to accomplish by sending an email to someone you're upset with?

- Do you want to make them aware of the fact they have upset you? That's easily accomplished with an angry email.
- Do you want to make them feel terrible and guilty so they change their behavior or beliefs? That can backfire. People are more likely to dig in than to recognize that they were wrong.
- Do you want to make sure this doesn't happen again? That will require level-headedness from both parties.

If you fire off a message based on your initial feelings, you'll probably only achieve the first of those objectives. That may create additional damage that you'll have to repair in the future.

If you're simply seething, write your first draft in a separate text file or in a journal—*not* in your email client. Then wait, ideally overnight. Return to what you hope to accomplish and decide what you really should say.

FIND THE RIGHT TONE

You may think you've cooled off and achieved a level tone, but remember that people regularly misinterpret tone in email.

Use the strategies from the previous chapter, "Writing the Tough Email":

- Run the message past a trusted colleague (for a "diplomacy check")
- Email it to yourself and see how it reads
- If you cannot get it right, consider whether email is the best medium for this conversation.

Remember that your email is permanent and not private. Even as you draft your response, imagine your manager or HR department reading it.

WHEN THERE IS NO HAPPY ENDING

If you have no realistic hope of improving the situation, you may need to simply write off that relationship or situation and move on, sadder and wiser.

If you need to keep working with the person who has upset you, consider having a fictional interaction with the recipient. Write two letters that you will *never* send. (Again, write them in a journal rather than on your corporate email account.)

First, write a letter or note to the other person outlining all the reasons you are upset or hurt and what they have done to wrong you.

Next, write back to yourself from the other person. This is where the fiction writing comes in. Pretend you are the person, and write yourself a message of apology. Then read it as many times as you need to.

The brain is wondrous and mysterious. Even though you know that *you've* written the response, the act of seeing the apology still sinks in. In creating this little email exchange, you make a fictional narrative of closure that, surprisingly, often helps in real life as well.

Just don't hit *Send*.

#30 REPLYING TOO QUICKLY

Do the people you work with expect responses to email within the hour? Or on the same day? How about people outside your team?

Often, the pressure to respond promptly comes from within. We sense unanswered emails hanging over our heads, generating anxiety. That's one reason we check them so frequently. Researchers have found people checking their email 70 times or more every day.

In an effort to clear out our inboxes, we pressure ourselves into replying quickly, even when the subject benefits from more thought. We end up committing to tasks we'd rather not do, or letting a good opportunity disappear because we are momentarily overwhelmed.

Worse, we propagate emails that don't further a productive exchange of ideas.

READ CAREFULLY BEFORE RESPONDING

How often has someone responded to you with a question that was answered later in the original message, thus generating a new email cycle, and possibly spawning copies of the same conversation to others?

Being quick to respond isn't useful if it's simply a token gesture. My friend Ivy B. Grey says, "A quick response has no value if it doesn't advance the work." If you skim a message quickly on your phone and fire off an immediate answer, you could discover that you misinterpreted the situation, or even the request.

BUY TIME FOR YOURSELF

If you're eager to please the people you work with, you'll say "yes" to too many things and stretch yourself too thin. Or, you might send a quick response that you later need to amend. I have learned through hard experience to take time to consider before committing to any major requests.

There's a middle ground between hitting *Snooze* and replying.

Rather than remaining silent when you receive a meaningful or thought-provoking request, learn the art of the noncommittal reply. Give yourself time to ponder without seeming unresponsive.

Here are examples that you can adapt for your needs:

I'll give this thought and get back to you by Wednesday at the latest.
This sounds fun. Let me figure out if I can balance it with my current workload and commitments. I'll let you know by the end of the week.

Then meet that commitment. Add the task to your schedule for the week.

Most people respect that you are giving their request or question careful consideration, even if they do not like your final answer.

NEVER FORWARD WITHOUT READING

We might think we can get an email out of our inbox by forwarding it to another person to take care of. That may be true, but read it carefully first. There may be personal or inappropriate content buried in the message.

#31 GETTING TANGLED IN THE THREAD

A while ago, someone responded to one of my biweekly Writing Practices emails by asking me to speak to his authors' group. I responded to his reply. He copied another person who was running the event. We arranged the event on an email chain anchored by that original, unrelated email about writing.

A couple of weeks later, I searched through my emails for the details of our arrangement. I couldn't find it. It finally showed up when I searched for the first name of the original respondent. I'd forgotten that the event details were tangled in that long email thread.

Conversations buried in unrelated email threads can get lost.

THE JOY—AND HASSLE—OF EMAIL THREADS

When you reply to an email, most email applications include the original text. (This is an option you can configure.) Each subsequent response adds to a growing chain. Email programs consolidate those various messages into one "thread" when displaying your mail. Instead of seeing multiple messages, one for each reply, you see one email subject with an indicator of how many messages are in the thread or conversation. This is great because it puts the whole conversation in one place.

But the threads can also hide things. As my story shows, important messages can get buried in a long thread. Here are a few ways to avoid failures due to long chains.

START A NEW THREAD WHEN THE SUBJECT CHANGES

When an email conversation turns to a new topic, or if you want to start a new subject, don't hijack the existing thread. Start a new one. (Clearly I should have done this for the speaking request.)

Your software may offer an option to split a conversation. Otherwise, start a new email message and conclude the old thread with a note that you are doing so.

Give the new message an appropriate subject line and copy the email addresses of only the people who need to be included in the new conversation. Everyone will thank you.

TRIM THE REPLIED CONTENT

Email software usually adds the content of the previous messages at the end of your reply. If the original content isn't relevant to the ongoing conversation or includes images and formatting, consider trimming the unnecessary material. This pares down the content sent back and forth and reduces the chance of vital information being lost in the shuffle.

#32 BUSINESS EMAILS IN PERSONAL TIME

Your emails carry another bit of information that you might not notice: the time you send them. Emails sent after normal "working hours" can telegraph messages you do not intend.

Some people check their email obsessively: late at night, first thing in the morning, and while on vacation. If you tackle your inbox during non-business hours, remember that people could see your emails arrive during those times. And that can lead to confusion, concern, or baseless worry. A cryptic email from your manager is no big deal at 10 on a Tuesday morning, but at 10 on a Friday night, it could ruin your entire weekend. Worse, people may sense that you expect them to always be on duty, especially people who report to you in an organization.

Countries and companies worldwide are responding to the stresses of email during off hours. In France, businesses cannot legally send employees emails during non-work hours. And some companies configure corporate email servers to automatically hold emails sent during nights and weekends until the start of the next business day.

If your company doesn't have that policy or if you work on

your own, like me, you can still make sure that you don't pressure others with the timing of your messages.

Delay the send. Does your email software have a "Send later" or "Schedule send" capability? If so, use it when you don't need the recipient to get the email until working hours.

Set expectations. Be explicit in the message body or the subject line about not expecting immediate responses.

Use the email signature. If you regularly work during strange hours, consider adding a message about that to your email signature. Here's an example from Toby Mildon, author of *Inclusive Growth* and a Diversity and Inclusion consultant:

> I am one of those people who works flexibly. I'm sending this email now because it suits how I balance my working hours. So, I don't expect that you will read, respond to, or act on this email outside of the hours that work for you.

Consider adding similar words to you own signature if you regularly work beyond office hours.

#33 EMAILING WHEN THERE'S A BETTER OPTION

Writing is a comfortable medium for me. Maybe you're the same. So I default to email for communicating with others. Recently, I've come to realize that email isn't always the best way to communicate, and clinging to it can be problematic.

We have many options available to us, including phone calls, video calls, messaging platforms, in-person meetings, and text messages. Email can also serve as the vehicle for non-written media: voice recordings or recorded videos and screen captures.

If you want to be truly effective in your business communications, think beyond the standard email message. Here are a few questions to consider as you evaluate which form to use.

DOES THE OTHER PERSON USE EMAIL FOR THIS TYPE OF COMMUNICATION?

Some prefer texting for friends and close colleagues, reserving email for more formal communications. For others, texting implies the need for an urgent reply. People have clear preferences for which channels they use for different kinds of messages.

If you communicate with someone regularly, clarify and set those expectations. Make sure you understand how an email will feel to this person—or if, indeed, they will even read it.

DOES THE TOPIC MERIT DISCUSSION WITH MULTIPLE PEOPLE?

If the topic would benefit from real-time, back-and-forth collaboration, consider scheduling a conference call or a meeting. This is doubly true if you need input from multiple people. Even with the hassle of getting on everyone's schedule, you'll spend less time coming to a resolution. Use email to set up the agenda for the discussion and share background material ahead of time.

SHOULD THE RECIPIENT READ IT CAREFULLY?

We tend to skim emails, even without realizing that we're skimming. When we're reading on a phone while doing other things, important details often escape us.

If you want someone to look carefully at the proposal or report you're sending them, consider putting it in a separate document and attaching the document to the message. It seems like unnecessary effort, but most of us look more closely at attachments.

ARE YOU TRYING TO DEMONSTRATE HOW TO DO SOMETHING?

My first job out of college was writing documentation for computer software. I learned two important lessons:

1. Writing clear procedural documentation is a skill that takes time to develop.
2. No one wants to read it anyway. They'll only look at the documentation once they've run into trouble.

There's a reason that YouTube is our favorite place to learn how to fix everything. It's easier to learn skills by watching than reading.

If you want to demonstrate how to do a task online, make a quick screen capture video. (Find recommendations in the Resources section on AnneJanzer.com.) If you're demonstrating a real-world task rather than an online one, make a quick video on your phone. Others will appreciate it, even if it's not a polished production. Making a quick video can be faster than crafting a carefully written message, and you'll save the recipient the effort of deciphering what you mean.

ARE YOU ASKING A FAVOR?

A study published in the *Journal of Experimental Social Psychology* had participants ask strangers to complete a survey. They made the request either in person or via email. Participants got much better results asking in person compared to email.

It's easier to get someone's attention in person, and perhaps harder for them to say no. If you have a favor to ask, you'll get better results asking them directly.

IS THE TONE IMPORTANT? ARE YOU SENDING BAD NEWS?

Do you have to give difficult feedback, or discuss a sensitive topic? In-person interactions are the safest when tone can be misinterpreted. Chapter #28, "Writing the Tough Email," outlines the challenges of communicating sensitive topics over email.

If possible, don't rely on written words alone.

If you cannot be there in person, try to get the other person on a video call. If you cannot do that and need to send a message, consider sending a short audio recording, which provides vocal inflection, or a video of yourself talking, which adds body language and facial expressions.

ARE YOU NAVIGATING LANGUAGE OR CULTURAL DIFFERENCES?

When people live halfway around the world, it's tempting to rely heavily on email. Arranging in-person calls requires resolving time zone differences. Someone is always getting up early or staying up late for those calls.

But language and cultural differences add even more opportunities for misunderstanding.

Especially when you are first forming a working relationship with a person halfway around the world, supplement email with phone or video conversations. If that doesn't work, consider adding a short video with your email message so your recipient can see the emotions and tone that you are trying to convey.

True email mastery includes knowing when not to use email at all.

P.S. THERE'S MORE

Writing a short book on a big topic is an exercise in deciding what to leave out. Head over to the Resources section of my website: AnneJanzer.com/Resources. Scroll down to find the cover of this book and you'll see a list of useful resources:

- Recommended reading and research, including the studies referred to in this book
- A list of useful tools related to the advice here, such as software for making quick screen videos
- A one-page summary of all the ways not to screw up your email

I'd love to hear from you as well.

Let me know what you thought of this book by ... wait for it ... sending me an email at Anne@AnneJanzer.com.

- Let others know what you think by leaving an honest review wherever you bought it. Reviews help other people find the book as well.

- Join my Writing Practices email list for every-other-week emails with writing inspiration or practical advice.

ACKNOWLEDGMENTS

This book would not exist without Melissa Wilson, who envisioned this series and invited me to participate. It is a fun journey, and I'm grateful to be part of it.

Many people shared their email failures and best practices with me. Only a small number found their way into these pages (this is a short book), but they *all* contributed to my understanding.

I owe sincere gratitude to everyone who let me share their stories and practices in these pages, including Karen Catlin, MB Deans, Douglas Burdett, Meredith Fidrocki, Maura Sullivan Hill, Stephan Hovnanian, Catherine Johns, Marti Konstant, Alastair McDermott, Toby Mildon, Evelyn Starr, and Pamela Wilson.

Sarah Tetlow offered expert guidance in good email management practices, and Lanie Denslow guided me through the nuances of cultural differences. I am grateful to the indefatigable Judy Dang for connecting me with both of those experts.

Early readers offered invaluable feedback and support,

including Meredith Fidrocki and Karen Catlin (who also contributed best practices), and Peri Caylor, who provided careful and detailed feedback. The Authoress community makes this whole venture feel much less lonely, and is a constant source of both inspiration and guidance.

The community of writers on my Writing Practices email list definitely helped to make this book better, and many of them appear in these pages, whether anonymously or through attribution. I must call out the contributions and support of a few of them: Peri Caylor, Carol Evanoff, William Gronke, Steven Hunt, Sarah Robison, Leica Torok, and Claire Wagner. I am grateful to everyone who reads and responds to my emails.

The LinkedIn community contributed insights and advice as well, including: Dan Gershenson, Roger C. Parker, Linda Popky, Nick Richtsmeier, Renee Rubin Ross, Krista Sewell, Darren Slade, Sunil Siri, Wilma Slenders, Judith Weber, Leslie Worthington, and many more.

My family contributed as well, from my brother John's cringe-worthy story of an email on a shared printer in the wrong place to my son Mark's recommendation for using videos to give feedback.

As with all of my books, Laurie Gibson and Mark Rhyns-burger are my 'safety net,' protecting me from writing-related embarrassment and making my books better for the readers.

And my thanks to my husband, Steve, for being the first reader and offering his constant and unfailing support and encouragement.

ABOUT THE AUTHOR

Anne Janzer is an award-winning author, nonfiction writing coach and unabashed writing geek committed to helping people make a positive impact with their writing. She supports and encourages writers and authors through her books, blog posts, webinars, and teaching.

Her writing-related books explore the science and practice of effective writing. They include *Get the Word Out, The Writer's Process, The Workplace Writer's Process,* and *Writing to Be Understood.* Those books have won awards from the Independent Publisher Book Awards, Foreword INDIES, and IndieReader Discovery.

Before she started writing books, Anne was a freelance marketing consultant, working with more than a hundred technology businesses to articulate positioning and messaging in crowded markets. This work led to her first book, *Subscription Marketing,* which has now had multiple editions and has been translated into multiple languages.

She lives on the Central Coast of California. Anne is a graduate of Stanford University.

Find out more or sign up for her every-other-week Writing Practices email list, at her website, AnneJanzer.com.

Printed in Great Britain
by Amazon

75173718R00068